Totally Strange Buildings

by Lisa M. Herrington

Content Consultant

Robbin Friedman, Children's Librarian
Chappaqua (N.Y.) Library

Reading Consultant

Jeanne M. Clidas, Ph.D.
Reading Specialistt

Children's Press®
An Imprint of Scholastic Inc.

Library of Congress Cataloging-in-Publication Data

Names: Herrington, Lisa M.
Title: Totally strange buildings/by Lisa M. Herrington.
Description: New York, NY: Children's Press, [2017] | Series: Rookie amazing
America | Includes index.
Identifiers: LCCN 2016030321| ISBN 9780531228975 (library binding) | ISBN
9780531225912 (pbk.)
Subjects: LCSH: Buildings—Miscellanea—Juvenile literature. | Structural
engineering—Juvenile literature.
Classification: LCC TH149 .H47 2017 | DDC 690—dc23
LC record available at https://lccn.loc.gov/2016030321

Produced by Spooky Cheetah Press

Printed in China 62

1 2 3 4 5 6 7 8 9 10 R 26 25 24 23 22 21 20 19 18 17

Photographs ©: cover: Douglas Keister; back cover: Design Pics Inc/Alamy Images; 3: TinaImages/
Shutterstock, Inc.; 4: MGH/Shutterstock, Inc.; 5: Christina Lundeen/Getty Images; 6: 3DSculptor/
iStockphoto; 7 main: Stefano Politi Markovina/Getty Images; 7 inset: View Pictures/UIG/Getty Images;
8-9 main: Arina P Habich/Shutterstock, Inc.; 9 left inset: Scott Prokop/Shutterstock, Inc.; 9 right inset:
Jeffrey Kaphan/Getty Images; 10-11: Clarence Martin/Dreamstime; 12: Geoff Kuchera/iStockphoto; 13:
tusharkoley/Shutterstock, Inc.; 14 right inset: Brett Beyer/Getty Images; 14 left inset: Lucas Jackson/
EPA/Newscom; 14-15 main: f11photo/Shutterstock, Inc.; 16-17: Allard Schager/Getty Images; 18-19:
Ricardo DeAratanha/Los Angeles Times/Getty Images; 20-21: UrbanTexture/Alamy Images; 22-23:
Douglas Keister; 24 inset: Education Images/UIG/Getty Images; 24-25 main: Design Pics Inc/Alamy
Images; 26-27 background: 123ducu/iStockphoto; 26 top left: tusharkoley/Shutterstock, Inc.; 26 top
center: f11photo/Shutterstock, Inc.; 26 top right: Ricardo DeAratanha/Los Angeles Times/Getty Images;
26 center left: Douglas Keister; 26 center: Stefano Politi Markovina/Getty Images; 26 center right: Design
Pics Inc/Alamy Images; 26 bottom left: MGH/Shutterstock, Inc.; 26 bottom center: UrbanTexture/Alamy
Images; 26 bottom right: Arina P Habich/Shutterstock, Inc.; 28-29 background: ooyoo/iStockphoto;
28 main: Wim Wiskerke/Alamy Images; 29 main: Nataliya Hora/Dreamstime; 30 main: alexsvirid/
Shutterstock, Inc.; 30 background: 123ducu/iStockphoto; 31 top: PeopleImages/iStockphoto; 31 bottom:
Allard Schager/Getty Images; 31 center bottom: MGH/Shutterstock, Inc.; 31 center top: f11photo/
Shutterstock, Inc.; 32: Douglas Keister.

Maps by Jim McMahon.

Table of Contents

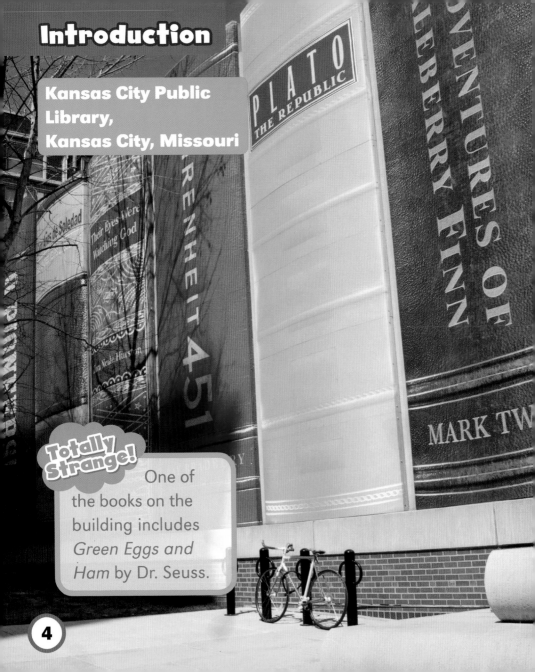

Introduction

Kansas City Public Library, Kansas City, Missouri

Totally Strange!

One of the books on the building includes *Green Eggs and Ham* by Dr. Seuss.

4

Is that a shelf from the world's biggest bookstore? No! It is the Kansas City Public Library. The walls of the parking garage look like giant book **spines**.

There are lots of amazing buildings across the United States. This library is just one of them. Let's explore more!

What Does It Look Like?

This building looks like a ship. It is the Walt Disney Concert Hall. Music concerts are held here.

The **architect** who designed the concert hall loves the sea. Do you think this building's curves look like the sails on a ship?

ship

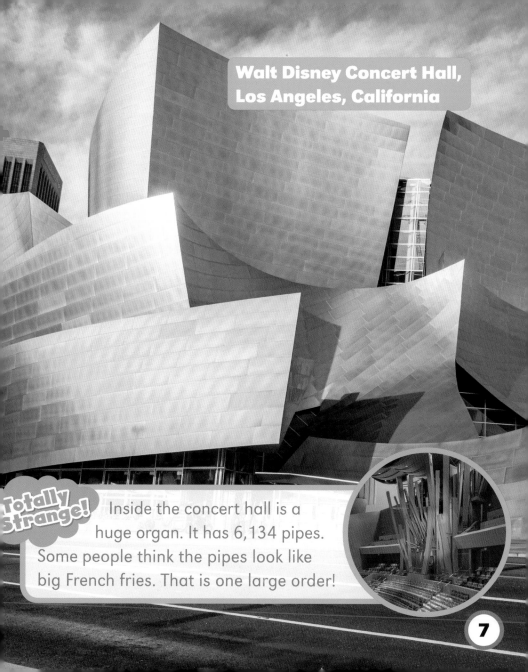

Walt Disney Concert Hall, Los Angeles, California

Totally Strange! Inside the concert hall is a huge organ. It has 6,134 pipes. Some people think the pipes look like big French fries. That is one large order!

Can you guess what this building is used for? It is an airport. Its roof is made of fabric triangles.

It was designed to match the shape of the nearby mountains.

Denver International Airport, Denver, Colorado

The triangles also look like American Indian teepees that were found nearby long ago.

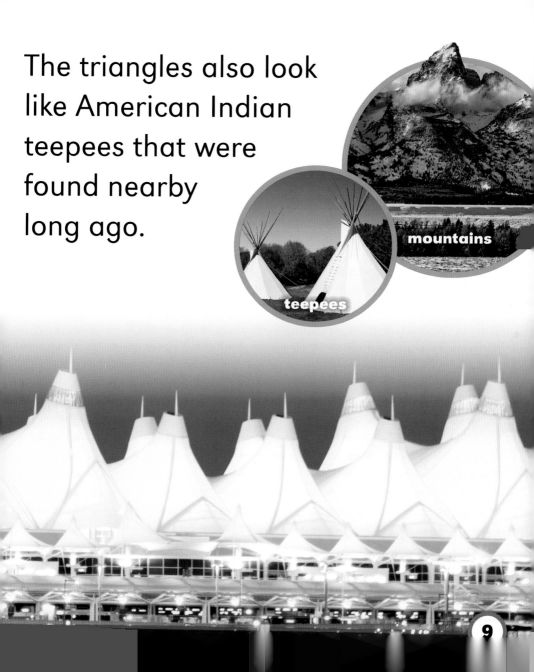

mountains

teepees

This building might make you think of picnics. It looks like the world's biggest basket! It used to be home to a basket-making company.

-LONGABERGER-

Skyscraper Superstars

The tallest buildings are known as **skyscrapers**. This one looks like a flying saucer! It is the Space Needle. It is 605 feet (184 meters) high. That is about as tall as 30 giraffes!

The Space Needle has an hourglass shape. A restaurant on top gives visitors a view of Seattle.

hourglass

**Space Needle,
Seattle, Washington**

**Totally
Strange!**

The Space
Needle was
built in just
400 days.

One of the most famous skyscrapers is One World Trade Center. It is the tallest building in the United States and the third tallest in the world. Nearly 10,000 workers took almost 10 years to build it. It opened in 2014.

One World Trade Center,
New York, New York

This building looks like
it is twisting as it rises.

spire ⟶

Totally Strange!

There is enough concrete in One World Trade Center to make a sidewalk from New York City to Chicago.

104 floors

12,774 windows

71 elevators

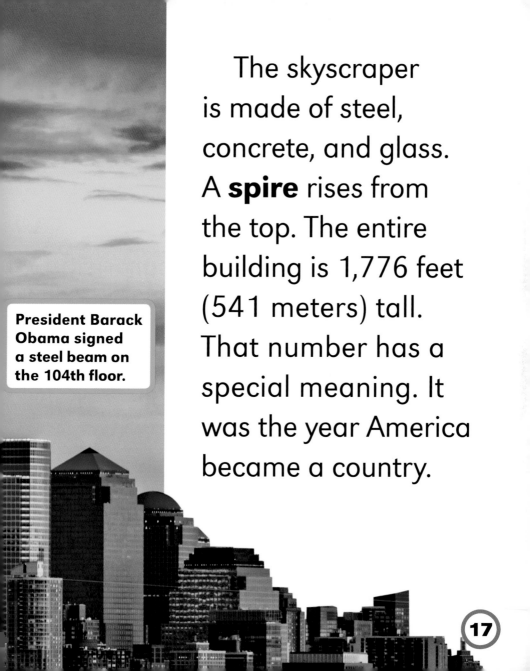

The skyscraper is made of steel, concrete, and glass. A **spire** rises from the top. The entire building is 1,776 feet (541 meters) tall. That number has a special meaning. It was the year America became a country.

President Barack Obama signed a steel beam on the 104th floor.

From Stone to Steel

Some buildings are in surprising places. This chapel is built into the red rocks of Arizona.

The Chapel of the Holy Cross stands on top of a hill. The spot was chosen for its peaceful views.

Chapel of the Holy Cross, Sedona, Arizona

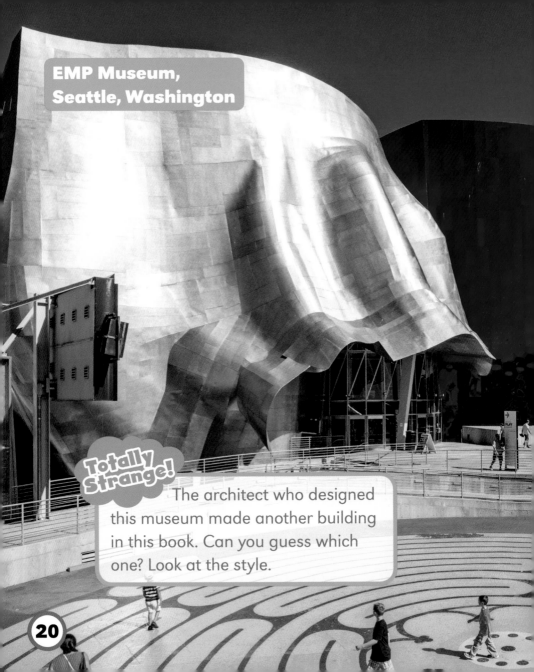

**EMP Museum,
Seattle, Washington**

Totally Strange!

The architect who designed this museum made another building in this book. Can you guess which one? Look at the style.

What a wild building! Visitors come to the EMP Museum to learn about music, movies, and more. The building is made from more than 21,000 metal pieces. Its curvy design is meant to show movement and energy.

Answer: Both the EMP Museum and the Walt Disney Concert Hall were designed by Frank Gehry.

Strange Houses and Museums

Once upon a time…someone built a storybook house.
This house looks like it is from a fairy tale.

Storybook houses like this one are made to be fun and playful. Snow White and the Seven Dwarfs could live here!

Storybook House, Olalla, Washington

What makes a storybook house?

pointy, uneven roof

odd-shaped doors and windows

stone walkway

23

Brrr...The inside of this hotel is made of ice and snow. The hotel is part of the Aurora Ice Museum.

The outside only looks like ice, though. Real ice would melt in warm weather.

inside the museum

Both inside and out, amazing buildings like this ice hotel are something to see!

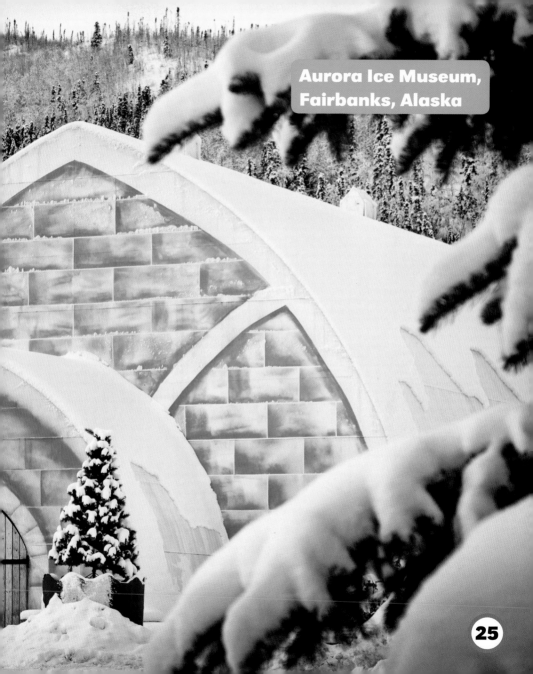

Aurora Ice Museum, Fairbanks, Alaska

United States

Can you find each of our totally strange buildings on the map below?

1 Space Needle

2 One World Trade Center

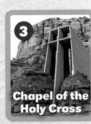
3 Chapel of the Holy Cross

4 Storybook House

5 Walt Disney Concert Hall

6 Aurora Ice Museum and Hotel

7 Kansas City Public Library

8 EMP Museum

9 Denver International Airport

1 8
4
Washington

Montana

Oregon

Idaho

Nevada

Utah

California

5

3
Arizona

Alaska
6

Hawaii

Alaska and Hawaii are not drawn to scale or placed in their proper places

of America

New Hampshire
Michigan
Vermont   Maine
North Dakota   Minnesota   Massachusetts
South Dakota   Wisconsin   New York   Rhode Island
Wyoming   Connecticut
Nebraska   Iowa   Ohio   Pennsylvania New Jersey
                          Illinois Indiana West Virginia Delaware
9   7   Maryland
Colorado   Kansas   Missouri   Kentucky   Virginia   Washington, D.C.
                                                         (U.S. capital)
                                              North Carolina
                          Tennessee
New Mexico   Oklahoma   Arkansas   South Carolina
                          Alabama
Texas   Georgia
           Louisiana
                      Mississippi   Florida

Compass Rose
North
West ◀◆▶ East
South

27

Haines Shoe House, Hellam, Pennsylvania

- A couple lives in this shoe house. The living room is in the toe. The kitchen is in the heel.

- A shoe salesman had the house made. It was created to look like a work boot.

- The house sits on Shoe House Road. It is open for tours and ice cream.

Strange?
You Decide!

WonderWorks, Orlando, Florida

- This wacky, upside-down building is an amusement park.

- Inside the building there are hurricane and earthquake rides.

- This building was designed to look like it was carried by a tornado and dropped on the side of a street.

You Name It

This building's design is a slam dunk! Can you guess which sport it honors?

Hint: *A gym teacher invented the sport in 1891. His students had to throw a ball into peach baskets.*

Answer: Basketball. The building is the Naismith Memorial Basketball Hall of Fame in Springfield, Massachusetts.

Glossary

- **architect** (AHR-kih-tekt): person who designs buildings and supervises the way they are built

- **skyscrapers** (SKY-skray-purz): very tall buildings

- **spines** (SPINES): on book covers, the part to which the pages are attached

- **spire** (SPIRE): structure that comes to a point at the top

Index

Facts for Now

Visit this Scholastic Web site for more information on
Strange Buildings:

www.factsfornow.scholastic.com

Enter the keywords Strange Buildings

About the Author

Lisa M. Herrington loves to write for children. She lives in a not-so-unusual house in Trumbull, Connecticut, with her husband and daughter.